SHORT WALKS FROM
East Sussex Pubs

Rupert Taylor

COUNTRYSIDE BOOKS
NEWBURY, BERKSHIRE

COUNTRYSIDE BOOKS
3 Catherine Road
Newbury, Berkshire

ISBN 1 85306 364 9

Designed by Mon Mohan
Cover illustration by Colin Doggett
Photographs and maps by the author

Produced through MRM Associates Ltd., Reading
Typeset by Paragon Typesetters, Queensferry, Clwyd
Printed by J. W. Arrowsmith Ltd., Bristol

Contents

Introduction   7

Walk 1   Chailey: The Five Bells (4 miles)   9

2   East Chiltington: The Jolly Sportsman (2 miles)   14

3   Barcombe Mills: The Anglers' Rest (2 miles)   19

4   Newick: The Bull (2½ miles)   24

5   Nutley: The William IV (3 miles)   28

6   Withyham: The Dorset Arms (2 miles)   32

7   Eridge: The Neville Crest and Gun (3 miles)   36

8   Mayfield: The Rose and Crown Inn (3 miles)   40

9   Warbleton: The War Bill-In-Tun (3 miles)   44

10   Chiddingly: The Gun (3 miles)   48

11   Milton Street: The Sussex Ox (2 miles)   52

12   East Dean: The Birling Gap Hotel (2 miles)   57

13   Wartling: The Lamb Inn (3½ miles)   62

14   Bodle Street Green: The White Horse Inn (3 miles)   66

15   Witherenden Hill: The Kicking Donkey
       (2 miles)   70

16   Ticehurst: The Bull (3 miles)   74

17   Salehurst: The Salehurst Halt (3 miles)   78

18   Ewhurst Green: The White Dog (2 miles)   82

19   Sedlescombe: The Queen's Head (4½ miles)   86

20   Udimore: The King's Head (3 miles)   90

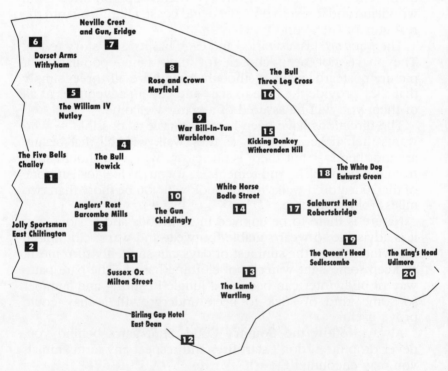

Area map showing locations of the walks.

Introduction

East Sussex is blessed with some of the finest countryside and some of the finest pubs in Britain. Put them both together and you have a combination that makes a delightful day out.

This book is not for the seasoned hiker who thinks 14 miles over rough terrain is a mere stroll. It is for people who believe the only way to see the country is on foot; for people who feel virtuous after taking some much-needed exercise and can reward themselves at the end (or the beginning) with a drink and perhaps something to eat.

None of the walks is too demanding, and everyone from toddlers to grannies should have energy to spare at the end of them. They cover the rich variety of landscape on offer, from woodland and forest to downland and coast, taking you into the real guts of the county.

The pubs are just as varied and each has its own story to tell. They have not been chosen for their fame, popularity or picture-postcard qualities, though some have all three; simply that they provide the base to start and end an adventure. At all of them you will be assured of a warm welcome.

The directions have been kept as simple as possible – who wants their nose in a book as they walk with all that beauty around them? – but there is no reason why you should stray from the right track. And remember, if you do feel lost, at none of the 20 featured walks in this book will you be more than two miles from your base.

Nature is there to be enjoyed in all moods and seasons, but it is advisable to wear suitable footwear and warm clothing in the winter. Even the sunniest of days can suddenly turn mean, so keep some light waterproof clothing handy. The bare pathway of midwinter can become a jungle in spring and summer so some kind of stick to keep undergrowth at bay could prove useful.

Always follow the Country Code. Shut gates behind you, never drop litter, don't start fires and respect any farm animals you may encounter.

In compiling these walks I owe both thanks and apologies.

Thanks to my wife Charlotte, who loyally strode beside me through fair and foul and always put us back on the right path when my map and the terrain seemed to be at odds; and apologies to the landlords (and landladies) who have had to deal with the effects of our muddy wellies.

Rupert Taylor
Spring 1995

Publisher's Note

We hope that you obtain considerable enjoyment from this book; great care has been taken in its preparation. However, changes of landlord and actual closures are sadly not uncommon. Likewise, although at the time of publication all routes followed public rights of way or permitted paths, diversion orders can be made and permissions withdrawn.

We cannot of course be held responsible for such diversion orders and any inaccuracies in the text which result from these or any other changes to the routes nor any damage which might result from walkers trespassing on private property. However, we are anxious that all details covering the walks and the pubs are kept up to date and would therefore welcome information from readers which would be relevant to future editions.

1 **Chailey**
The Five Bells

The annual beating the bounds of Chailey is not a job for the faint-hearted. The border stretches for nearly 24 miles, making it one of the largest parishes in the county. The Five Bells, a handsome old building was built in 1490 as a private dwelling and became a public house in the 17th century. It took its name from the number of bells in the parish church nearby, though no change was considered necessary by the landlord when the church added a sixth in 1810.

Like most old pubs, it has a resident ghost but the most chilling encounter is likely to be made in the spacious main bar area, where a portrait of local magistrate Lord Tuppen (1658-1739) smiles down on the clientele. The benign countenance belies a steely nature, for when he was 'the beak' Lord Tuppen believed in the motto 'steal and you will hang'. He carried it through to the letter. According to local records more than 500 men were sent to the gallows for anything from stealing bread to murder.

The large beer garden is fully equipped to keep children amused, whether they like swinging, sliding or climbing. They may even spot the odd chicken wandering around – temporary absconders from the little run at the front of the pub. If the weather is unkind, there is a family room and play area indoors, well stocked with toys. There is an excellent range of home-made food at this Whitbread pub, with a strong emphasis on fish dishes: swordfish steaks, plaice, halibut and salmon. Alternatively, there is traditional liver and bacon casserole or the exotic Thai beef, while vegetarians are well catered for with dishes such as vegetable tikka. The range of beers includes Boddingtons, Wadworth 6X and Whitbread Summer Ale. The pub is open all day from Monday to Saturday, 11 am to 11 pm, and on Sunday from 12 noon to 10.30 pm.

Telephone: 01825 722259.

How to get there: Chailey stands on the main A275 road between Lewes and East Grinstead, and the Five Bells is just south of the village green. Don't be confused by North and South Chailey, a couple of miles or so either side of the old village.

Parking: There is ample car parking space in front of the pub. You can also leave your car at the church car park.

Length of the walk: 4 miles. Map: OS Landranger 198 Brighton and the Downs (inn GR 182391).

This is a walk with three different features: common land rich in bracken and silver birch, dense ancient woodland and wide open countryside with magnificent views.

The Walk

From the Five Bells, look for the footpath sign immediately opposite the pub entrance on the far side of the main road and wander under the line of horse chestnut trees parallel with the A275 until you are opposite the parish hall on your right. Here the path turns left, over a stile and across a field to another beneath a massive oak. Bear diagonally right, climbing a gentle

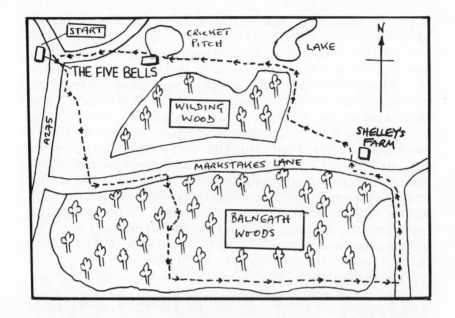

slope until you see the half-timbered outline of Furzeley Farm among the trees in the distance. Make for the farm and you will come to a gate and join Markstakes Lane.

Turn left along the lane and continue for about a quarter of a mile under the canopy of trees and with a flint wall on your right. Then it's into the sticks again with the footpath clearly marked on the right beside a cottage. The terrain changes to an open common and you are faced with three choices – opt for the pathway to the left and climb gently. This stretch of common is the smaller sister of North Chailey's breezy nature reserve, and is itself alive with butterflies in the summer. The treeline marks the end of the climb after about 500 yards and you descend gradually through Balneath Wood, a delightful mixture of oak, beech, hornbeam and massive holly bushes. Under a particularly gnarled hornbeam the path veers sharply left and takes you down to Balneath Lane and the edge of the wood.

Before reflecting that it is not a lane at all, but an ancient droveway, drink in the view of the South Downs in front of you – Black Cap in the west and Firle Beacon in the east. Turn left

11

along the lane and see how subtly that view can change as you progress. After half a mile you come to Deadmantree Lane and turn left, a sinister name for a quiet road sprinkled on the right with old cottages and everywhere, in spring and summer, with wild flowers. You may see clumps of a wild plant known as butcher's broom, which the gipsies spray with gold and sell as a lucky charm.

It is half a mile to the road junction with Markstakes Lane, where you bear left and look out for a half-hidden pathway located about 400 yards along the road. It is on the right-hand side, just beyond Shelley's Farm, which boasts an old-fashioned plough as lawn decoration, and will take you past a tennis court and across a paddock. From here the path crosses a field and a stream, and you stick close to the edge of the copse which climbs upwards beneath Wilding Wood to a kidney-shaped lake and a peaceful spot for anglers.

Turn left beside the lake. Your way lies across the field and you should be able to make out a signpost on the horizon. If you haven't got 20:20 vision, never mind. Just keep a distant rotten oak tree to your right front, its bare branches clawing at the sky like an agonised hand.

If you think the footpath is now entering someone's garden, you are right, but it is a brief passage past the shrubbery. When the path becomes a metalled track it takes you alongside what must surely be the smallest cricket pitch in the county, complete with a doll's house of a pavilion. This is the home ground of the Priory Ruins XI and, ruined or not, boundaries can be achieved with a gentle tap. When out of range of the lustier blows, you will see the lane that leads to Cornwells Bank in front of you. Bear left and the Five Bells will become visible after about 200 yards.

Places of interest nearby
The Bluebell Railway, Sheffield Park is five miles away on the A275 between East Grinstead and Lewes. Vintage steam trains chug through the Sussex countryside to Horsted Keynes and Newcombe Bridge – the Bluebell Railway has the largest collection in the south, dating from 1865 to 1958. Every weekend and daily May to September. Telephone: 01825 722370 (talking timetable) or 01825 723777 (enquiries). *Sheffield*

The Bluebell Railway.

Park Garden nearby, is a 100-acre landscaped garden originally laid out by 'Capability' Brown in the 18th century. Now owned by the National Trust, the garden features many rare trees and is set around five lakes linked by cascades. Telephone: 01825 790655.

East Chiltington
The Jolly Sportsman

2

Pubs are an essential part of any community, where local affairs are invariably debated night after night. But they are rarely an essential part of grass roots democracy where the conclusions from those debates actually carry some weight. Such was the case at the Jolly Sportsman, which was until recent times the meeting place of the parish council (all seven of them). It also serves as a polling station whenever there is an election. One year, when an election inconveniently occurred when there was a change of licensee, the room was not available and the electorate of 293 had to make their way to a barn to cast their votes. The pub, still remembered as the Old Thatch by more senior members of the community, also served as a village shop until trade dropped to a trickle and it was forced to close.

One of the great joys of the Jolly Sportsman is the garden, alive with flowers from early spring until late autumn. It's a great place to sit at a bench and enjoy the totally rural setting, with views to the downs, and children will appreciate the range

of play equipment which includes a giant wooden 'stockade'. Inside, there's a cosy bar, a games room and a dining area. A versatile range of foods is on offer at this freehouse, from simple ploughman's and salads to more elaborate fish dishes, curries and home-made pies. The King and Barnes Brewery at Horsham provides the bitter, and you can also select from John Smith's, Young's Special and Wadworth 6X. Harveys Old is a favourite in the winter months. Lager comes in the shape of Fosters and Kronenbourg, and there is Dry Blackthorn on draught for cider lovers. There is no objection to children and well-behaved dogs. The Jolly Sportsman is closed on Mondays. It is open Tuesday to Saturday from 11.30 am to 2.30 pm and 6 pm to 11 pm during the summer, 7 pm to 11 pm in the winter, and from 12 noon to 3 pm and 7 pm to 10.30 pm on Sundays.
Telephone: 01273 890400.

How to get there: East Chiltington is signposted from the B2116 Ditchling road. From Novington Lane, follow the Jolly Sportsman sign into Chapel Lane, where you will find the pub on your left.

Parking: There is a large car park to the side of the pub and additional parking in the lane outside.

Length of the walk: 2 miles. Map: OS Landranger 198 Brighton and the Downs (inn GR 153374).

Only for about a third of a mile will you feel earth under your feet, but this is essentially a rural walk, beside woodland and hedgerow – with some interesting local history thrown in for good measure.

The Walk
Turn left from the pub and climb Chapel Lane until you reach the 12th century village church. Turn left again and descend the track to Stantons Farm. This was the home in the 19th century of Susannah Stacey, better known as Grandma, who was by any measure a remarkable woman – cook and counsellor, friend to the poor and sick, a healer through strange herbal potions. She was a curious mixture of well-bred Victorian lady and white witch. Stantons became a place of pilgrimage for those troubled

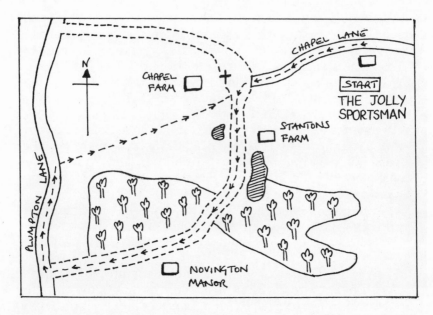

in mind or body and Grandma's advice and medicines were never denied them.

Opposite the old farm is what appears to be an even older barn, leaning in places at gravity-defying angles. It is strange how local oral tradition can bring a fairly insignificant moment in time to life. A troop of Cromwellian Roundheads were quartered in the barn during the English Civil War. Gaze at the venerable building and you can almost see them.

Follow the track as it winds through the trees, passing the iron gateway to Novington Manor on your left. It was specially commissioned and created in Italy more than a century ago and its intricacy commands attention. The track emerges after a mile in Plumpton Lane and facing you is a house called The Rest. It looks an unremarkable, solid Edwardian home – but in the 1930s it was the scene of terror. Nationally renowned veterinary surgeon Major Arthur Farrant lived here and he became the target of a bizarre murder attempt. Someone laced his coffee with strychnine and put rat poison in his water tank. Happily, the good Major survived, but the Plumpton poisoner was never caught.

Turn right in Plumpton Lane and continue for about 500

The timbered barn at Stantons Farm.

yards until you see a path leading off to the right. It goes through a commercial sand pit and then continues diagonally across the fields to East Chiltington church. Away to the left is Plumpton racecourse. It can be an uncanny sensation on race days to be in the middle of peaceful countryside and suddenly hear the urgent echoes of the loudspeaker system and the roars of a distant multitude.

Take a look to the right and you will see a downland landmark, and perhaps two. On the steep escarpment stands a wood in the shape of a 'V', planted in 1887 to mark Queen Victoria's golden jubilee. A little to the left of it, if the sun is casting the right shadow, spot the cross carved in the hillside. You can walk across it and not know it is there because it is now totally overgrown, but it once guided Crusaders to the point over the hills for the coast and the distant Holy Land.

Having rejoined the track at the church it is simply a question of retracing your steps back down the hill to the Jolly Sportsman.

Places of interest nearby

Lewes Castle (five miles). The keep of this Norman stronghold dominates the town and there is also an early 14th century barbican gateway. Combined tickets can be bought to view the castle, the Lewes Living History model and the Museum of Sussex Archaeology. Open all year except December 25 and 26. Monday to Saturday 10 am to 5.30 pm (or dusk if earlier), Sunday and bank holidays 11 am to 5.30 pm (or dusk if earlier). Telephone: 01273 486290.

③ Barcombe Mills
The Anglers' Rest

The pub used to be the Station Hotel, built in the middle of the 19th century when the railway came to Barcombe. The railway is no more, but anglers certainly are and so the name was changed.

The walls of the spacious, L-shaped bar are decorated with old pictures of the place that gave Barcombe Mills its name. The flour mill that stood by the river Ouse was mentioned in Domesday and the last working mill was built on the site in 1870. It stood empty for many years after ceasing to grind corn until 1934 when it became a button factory, owned by a German and run by Italians as one of the major sources of employment in the village. But the war clouds were looming and the factory was completely destroyed by a mysterious fire in the early hours of Friday, 10th March, 1939. Sadly, several of the Italians who worked here died when the ship carrying them back to their native country was torpedoed by a German U-boat shortly after the outbreak of the Second World War. Their ghosts are supposed to haunt the site of the old mill.

Five real ales are always on offer at this freehouse, the constant being Harveys supported, perhaps, by Adnams Broadside or Brakspear. The renowned Timmy Taylor's Landlord is also a regular visitor.

There are at least three dozen recipes on offer at the Anglers' Rest and the menu is constantly changing. Home-made pies include steak and mushroom, steak and kidney and rabbit, while vegetarians are well catered for with the likes of garlic mushroom pie and cheese and broccoli pancakes. They are big on traditional puddings here, too, with spotted dick and treacle pudding, among others, always on the menu. It is worth noting that the pub is closed at lunchtime on Monday, and on Mondays, Tuesdays and Wednesdays only bar snacks are available. They have a traditional roast at lunchtime on Sunday but there is no food on Sunday evenings. There is a large beer garden at the rear, with a covered patio area and tables and benches, and children will delight in the Wendy house on the lawn – a sophisticated, two-floor property. They are welcome inside the pub, as are well-behaved dogs. The pub is open Monday 6 pm to 11 pm, Tuesday to Friday 11.30 am to 2.30 pm and 6 pm to 11 pm; Saturday 11.30 am to 3 pm and 6 pm to 11 pm; and Sunday 12 noon to 3 pm and 7 pm to 10.30 pm.

Telephone: 01273 400270.

How to get there: The three parts of the village (Barcombe, Barcombe Cross and Barcombe Mills) stand close together about 5 miles north of Lewes. Barcombe Mills lies furthest east and is best reached from the A26 Lewes road where the turning is clearly signposted at Clay Hill.

Parking: The car park is wide and deep, running to the right of the pub.

Length of the walk: 2 miles. Map: OS Landranger 198 Brighton and the Downs (inn GR 150428).

An enjoyable riverside walk that is almost a journey back in time. It takes in a Roman road, a vanished railway, a vanished rural industry and a vanished

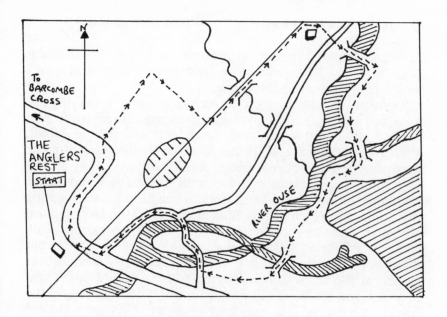

threat – when Hitler was poised on the other side of the Channel with an invasion force, pill boxes sprouted like mushrooms beside the river Ouse. Operation Sealion never happened, but the fortifications remain. Count how many you can see.

The Walk

Turn left out of the pub and climb steep Crink Hill, a 90-degree kink in the road. When it bends back into shape again there is a footpath leading straight ahead from the lane. Follow it across the field and turn sharply right at the hedge. Stick to the hedge and you will come to the dismantled railway line. It connected Lewes with Uckfield and beyond, but was axed in the 1960s. Turn left and enjoy the broad, flat solid path that has been left behind, with open countryside on every side and the downs at your back. Just before you go over the railway bridge over Bevern Stream is the point where you cross the course of the old Roman road. There is not much evidence of it (except later in the walk) but it runs straight as an arrow from the Lewes area deep into the Weald.

21

The river Ouse at Barcombe Mills.

Some 200 yards beyond the bridge you will come to a cluster of houses, and the footpath branches off to the right here. This was once a popular spot for boating; boats could be hired from a café beside the river and paddled downriver, a rival to the Anchor Inn further north whose patrons paddled upriver. Café and boats have now long gone from here. There is a barn in front of you and the path runs to the right of it, crossing the Ouse over a wooden bridge. Turn right on the far bank and stick to the river as it drifts lazily towards distant Lewes, Newhaven and the sea, negotiating a couple of bridges along your way.

Shortly the surround of Barcombe reservoir will come into view – the expanse of water shielded behind a tall grassy bank. The path runs between reservoir and river before you branch to the right and cross another long bridge toward a solid track and the entrance to the site of the old mills. This is a place of excitement: bridges, weirs and rushing water among great old trees. In late Victorian times this was a popular Sunday destination for Lewes folk, who travelled the short distance on the railway and enjoyed picnics here. Turn right when you join the track and follow it to a squat little building which was once the toll house. It was the first place in Sussex where road tolls were levied and was around at the time of the Norman Conquest. But it seems to be in the middle of nowhere – and that's where the Roman road comes in.

Follow the track off to the left until it joins Barcombe Mills Road and turn right, past Barcombe Mills station (now a café and restaurant) to the Anglers' Rest beside it.

Places of interest nearby
Boating on the river Ouse from the *Anchor Inn*, Boast Lane, Barcombe (two miles). Boats are available for hire from spring through to autumn for trips up the river. Telephone: 01273 400414.

4 Newick
The Bull

The Bull Inn can trace its history back to 1510 when it was built specifically as a place of rest and refreshment. It served the pilgrims travelling between the cathedrals and shrines of Winchester, Chichester and Canterbury. The name came not from the animal but from the original sign of a rolled sheet of parchment to indicate a papal bull or edict. It is a fascinating old building, fronting the village green, packed with architectural gems, atmosphere... and ghosts. There's the humanoid figure that people get a fleeting glimpse of, flitting along the restaurant wall and disappearing into thin air at the window, the icy room upstairs that pet animals won't go near, and the grinning old lady who so startled one of the cooks in the kitchen that she picked up her skirts and ran.

The menu is extensive and the Bull has built an enviable reputation for food. There are simple bar meals like pies and jacket potatoes, and feasts featuring 15 different starters and a range of delights to follow that includes game in season. Vegetarian dishes figure prominently, too. Meals can be eaten in the massive main bar with its inglenook fireplace or in the restaurant. Harveys, John Smith's, 6X and Directors are featured at this Courage inn, with a full range of lagers, Guinness and cider. You can watch the parish pump, dating from Queen Victoria's diamond jubilee celebrations in 1897, grow a few minutes older from benches at the front of the Bull, or relax in the courtyard beer garden at the rear. Children and dogs are equally welcome inside. The Bull is open Monday to Saturday 11 am to 3 pm and 6 pm to 11 pm; and Sunday 12 noon to 3 pm and 7 pm to 10 pm.

Telephone: 01825 722055.

How to get there: Newick lies on the A272 between Uckfield and Haywards Heath. It is about 8 miles north of Lewes.

Parking: There is a car park behind the pub. Alternatively you can park at the side of the lane outside.

Length of the walk: 2 ½ miles. Map: OS Landranger 198 Brighton and the Downs (inn GR 418213).

A walk that incorporates the best of this historic village, open countryside and riverside. The views on all sides are idyllic.

The Walk
From the pub turn right into Church Road and admire the attractive mixture of buildings. Note the house with the trompel'oeil feature at the front. In the days of window tax, people filled in their windows; this one has a window painted over the filled-in area.

After about 200 yards, beyond two further pubs (Newick is rich in pubs), turn left to the church of mellow stone and weather-worn carved faces beside the door and pass by the right-hand side of it through the churchyard. The path continues over the wall at the end and out across an open field to the corner of Founthill Wood where you cross a stile. Keeping a small stream on your right and a dome-like hillock on your left, continue in a straight line to a charming lake, complete with its own island where two inhabitants would be a crowd. The

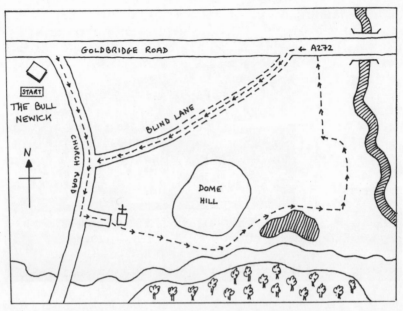

way lies through the gap into the field ahead with its distant view of the river and attendant alder trees.

Stick close to the edge of the field and follow it round to the left. The Ouse, with its curiously named Eel Pot curve, Hanger Wood and ox bow lake, remains to your right at the bottom of the fields. Follow the pathway as it turns its back on the river and turn right at the first available gap on to a long, straight track leading to the A259 west of Gold Bridge. Join the main road briefly (there is a wide verge), turning left and going past a gate on your left. Just beyond it, keep your eyes peeled for Blind Lane, a tantalisingly narrow entrance where the view of the path ahead is quickly swallowed-up by trees and undergrowth.

The old turnpike toll house still stands beside the main road and Blind Lane may well have got its name from the toll dodgers, who used it to keep out of sight of the toll house and hence avoid the payments, which could well be hefty: 'For every horse or other beast drawing a coach 6d. (2½p); for 1st horse or other beast drawing a wagon 7½d. and for every other beast 5d. For a dog or goat drawing any carriage 1d. Drove of oxen cows or cattle 10d. per score; sheep, calves or swine 5d. per score. For every vehicle moved by steam, gas or mechanism

26

A nearby house with a 'disguised' blank window.

5s. (25p).' Tolls were doubled in the winter months for all laden vehicles.

The path undergoes a steady change during its ¼ mile course to Newick, growing into a wide track and then a solid lane with high hedges on either side. Blind Lane enters Church Road just north of the church itself. Turn right and retrace your steps to the Bull.

Places of interest nearby

Barkham Manor Vineyard and Great Barn at Piltdown is two miles away on the A272 between Haywards Heath and Uckfield. International award-winning wines are grown where the notorious Piltdown Man was discovered. There are self-guided tours of the vineyard and modern winery with wine tastings. Open April to December, Tuesday to Saturday 10 am to 5 pm, Sunday and bank holidays 11 am to 5 pm. Telephone: 01825 722103.

⑤ Nutley
The William IV

They are wild about the Wild West in Nutley, which became a mecca for Red Indian enthusiasts with an annual pow-wow at the village. Nutley itself has the feel of a frontier town on a smaller scale, with Ashdown Forest closing in on all sides, beautiful but untamed. Perhaps it is just coincidence that one of the pub's great attractions is Fort Apache in the gardens. It is a complete timber Wild West town for youngsters, extending over seven acres and complete with sheriff's office, jail, saloon, corral and tree house 'lookout'.

While Fort Apache keeps the children occupied, grown-ups can make the most of a huge menu and a wide range of beers. The line-up changes all the time but just a few of the regulars are Charles Wells Bombardier Bitter, Old Peculier, Harveys, HSB, Abbot and William Younger. There are two varieties of stout and cider. The food extends from a simple soup and a roll to a full three-course meal with an exciting range to choose from. It can be enjoyed in the saloon or the public bar (the latter so comfortably furnished it looks like a living room) or in the Buffs Room restaurant. The William IV has one of the best bar billiards tables in the county and its regulars are also enthusiastic members of the local crib and darts leagues. Children and dogs are equally welcome inside.

How the pub got its name, incidentally, remains a mystery. It was not built until about a century after the monarch's death and as far as anyone knows he had no connection with the village. He probably would not want one, either. The Sussex historian Mark Antony Lower denounced the forest dwellers as rogues and vagabonds.

The pub is open all day on Saturday, and Monday to Friday from 10.30 am to 3 pm and 5.30 pm to 11 pm; and Sunday from 12 noon to 3 pm and 7 pm to 10.30 pm.

Telephone: 01825 712671.

How to get there: Nutley straddles the A22 about halfway between Uckfield and East Grinstead. The pub stands at the southern end of the village, opposite the playing field.

Parking: There is a large car park extending across the front and one side of the pub.

Length of the walk: 3 miles. Map: OS Landranger 198 Brighton and the Downs (inn GR 273444).

Ashdown Forest is an invigorating place at any time of the year, wild rolling acres that still occupy a sizeable chunk of East Sussex where nature has not been reduced to placid obedience. There are few pubs with close proximity to the forest, but it laps at the garden fence of the William IV and offers walkers a flavour of a secret world apart while never straying more than a mile from civilization.

The Walk

Turn left out of the pub car park beside the A22 then almost immediately left again. There is a bewildering selection of pathways leading off into the undergrowth, but you continue straight on down the hill. On the horizon is what appears to be a castle tower straight out of a fairytale – this is, in fact, Fairwarp church, standing serene and alone beside the great forest.

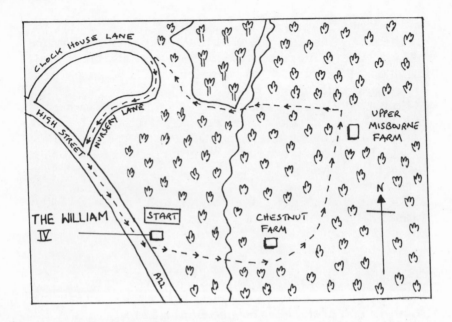

Your route takes you past Chestnut Farm on the left and the pathway is bedecked with wild flowers in spring and summer and massive toadstools in autumn. Fly mushrooms (*Amanita Muscaria*) the size of dinner plates predominate here, bright red with white spots to provide a spectacular but poisonous decoration to the pathway.

Just beyond Chestnut Farm the way leads over a stile and dives into woodland of silver birch and hornbeam, which gradually thins as the path twists to the left and you find yourself on the forest proper, with sweeping vistas of bracken and gorse. It's an old Sussex saying that when the gorse is in bloom it's the season for kissing. Not such a daft anecdote – the gorse is always in bloom. The coconut aroma from the bushes excites the olfactory sense, just as the undulations of Ashdown attract the visual one.

The route back towards the pub, now on the other side of the valley to your left, is an obvious one – a track at least 20 yards wide going dead straight down the hill from the back of Upper Misbourne Farm. At the bottom it enters a patch of woodland and crosses a stream. Under the dark branches, particularly in

A meandering track in Ashdown Forest.

the fading light of winter's afternoon, it is easy to believe in the local legend of a headless ghost. A smuggler had his head shot off in a fight with the King's men, and his spirit wanders the forest with a lantern, searching for the spot where he hid his kegs of brandy before coming to such an unfortunate end.

From the stream you bear right along a narrow pathway that hugs the hillside, climbing for about 300 yards until you reach the roadway at Clock House Lane. Turn left and follow the road as it doubles back on itself and becomes Nursery Lane. After 200 yards it joins the main road at Nutley post office. Turn left and make your way down the village High Street for about 400 yards to the William IV on your left.

Places of interest nearby
Barnsgate Manor Vineyard, Herons Ghyll (three miles) is on the A26 between Uckfield and Crowborough. A 12-acre vineyard with walks, winery, wine museum and a herd of llamas. Open all year, daily, 10 am to 5 pm. Telephone: 01825 713366.

6 Withyham
The Dorset Arms

The pub dates from the 15th century and used to be a farm-house. It takes its name from the Sackville family of Buckhurst, who became earls of Dorset in 1604. Some 70 years later one Isaac Rogers found himself in trouble at the Quarter Sessions for keeping an illegal alehouse at Withyham – presumably the Dorset Arms. He admitted 'total ignorance of the laws and statutes of the kingdom', said he was 'very sickly by nature' and only sold beer to keep himself and his family from being a burden on the parish. Maybe Isaac got away with it, because the pub has been providing rest and refreshment for centuries.

Today you can rest and refresh in style. There is a cosy bar where you can buy ploughman's lunches, salads, sandwiches and jacket potatoes, or you can take your seat in the à la carte restaurant where the comprehensive list of home-cooked fare includes steaks, chicken dishes, pies and seafood. Sunday lunch with all the trimmings is a particular success. The bar still retains the huge open fireplace in front of which a vestry meeting was held in 1820 to which poor parents of children of 11 years of age or more were summoned 'to order the putting out of such children to service'.

There's a benevolent ghost who replaces blazing logs if they fall out of the fire, and strange things happened when the funeral of a former landlady was held here. All the lights went out in the kitchen, where she had spent much of her time, and then they came on and off again in a steady, pulsing rhythm.

This is a Harveys pub and in addition to the bronze nectar from Lewes you can sample Carling and Tennents lagers and cider in the form of Scrumpy Jack and Strongbow. Children and dogs are actively encouraged to pay a visit and there is a big beer garden for them both to roam about in. The Dorset Arms is open Monday to Friday 11.30 am to 3 pm, and 5.30 pm to 11 pm; Saturday 11 am to 3 pm and 6 pm to 11 pm; and Sunday 12 noon to 3 pm and 7 pm to 10 pm.

Telephone: 01892 770278.

How to get there: Withyham lies about 3 miles north-west of Crowborough on the B2110 linking Tunbridge Wells and East Grinstead.

Parking: There is ample room in the pub's own car park or in the lane alongside.

Length of the walk: 2 miles. Map: OS Landranger 188 Tunbridge Wells (inn GR 356497).

The writer E.V. Lucas described Withyham as the Jewel of Sussex. It is easy to see why. There is not much to the village itself, the pub, the church, a few houses grand and small, but its situation among rolling hills and woodland is glorious. This walk takes in just some of these geographical features and views.

The Walk

Go past the little green facing the pub and continue along the side of the B2110. Towering above you on the left is the village church and it is worth making a detour (and getting out of breath on the steep climb) to admire. The building contains many memorials to the Sackville and de la Warr families, the

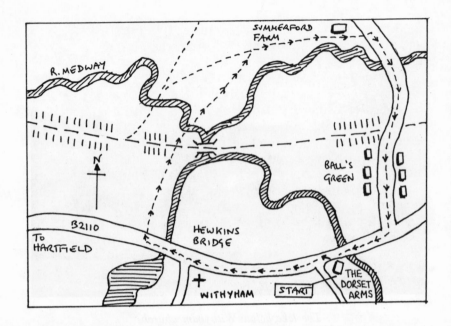

most impressive being Caius Cibber's sculptured monument to Thomas Sackville, who died in 1677 at the age of 13. The life size marble figures of his parents, in contemporary dress, kneel on cushions gazing sadly at the boy, who reclines holding a skull (to signify death in infancy). It is said the steps of black stone on which the table tomb is raised act as a barometer. If they bear signs of damp, as if they have recently been washed, then a change in the weather is on the way. In the church, too, lie the ashes of authoress and poet Vita Sackville-West, who was born at Knole and died at Sissinghurst in 1962. She was the wife of historian Harold Nicolson.

Continue along the B2110 over Hewkins Bridge, where it crosses a tributary of the river Medway, and look across the lake in front of you to Hartfield's spire piercing the distant woodland. Immediately after the bridge you come to a footpath leading off to the right. Follow it, keeping the stream to your right, and approach the dismantled railway which once linked Groombridge with East Grinstead and is now the Forest Way Country Park walk. Go over the old line and then cross the Medway proper via a bridge.

The lake below Withyham church.

The path bears right and climbs away from the water for about 600 yards before linking up with a broad track that leads past Summerford Farm. Turn right into Station Road and pass through the hamlet of Ball's Green. Soon after passing the school you rejoin the B2110. Turn right and go down the hill for about 300 yards when you will see the Dorset Arms on your left.

Places of interest nearby

Poohsticks Bridge can be found one mile off the A264 between East Grinstead and Tunbridge Wells at Hartfield. The site was immortalised by A.A. Milne in his tales of Christopher Robin, Winnie the Pooh et al.

Eridge
7 The Neville Crest and Gun

Everywhere you look in the village of Eridge, and for a radius of several miles, you will see a striking heraldic device on the houses, cottages and lodges: a bull with a Tudor rose and portcullis and a large 'A' tied with tassels. This is the emblem of the Marquess of Abergavenny, family name Neville, who holds the sway in Eridge Park. The pub takes half its name from the family and boasts a beautifully painted bull on the front wall. But where does the gun come in? Apparently the building is 500 years old and used to be a row of houses called Gunsmith's Cottages. They cast a cannon here in 1768 which stood on the little village green for many years and was fired, with suitable ceremony, to celebrate high days and holidays. There is a picture of it in the pub's restaurant.

Behind the Neville Crest and Gun's rose pink old bricks and creepers lies a fascinating interior of low beams and interesting angles. Always to be found at the bar is Neville, a stuffed brown bear with a chequered past. Neville was a dancing bear in

Turkey, entertaining the crowds at markets and fairs. When he died some 50 years ago, his skin was exported to England as a rug. The new owners wanted more than a rug and had him stuffed – not particularly successfully because Neville had no hands, no feet, no tail, no ears, a shortage of teeth and the wrong-coloured eyes. The licensees recently put all this right, restoring Neville to the glory of his dancing days.

This Whitbread house served as a coaching inn for many years and the coach-house and stables still stand. The latter are said to be haunted by the ghost of a girl raped and then murdered by one of the stablehands early in the 19th century.

No fewer than 24 real ales are available here and the choice is always changing. Not surprisingly, it has become a popular venue for beer festivals. The range of home-made food is extensive and there is something to please all tastes. You can eat in the bar or in the restaurant, which seats 100, and there is ample provision front and rear for those who prefer the open air. Breakfast has become a feature here in recent times. The pub is geared to children, with a bouncy castle in the grounds and an impressive looking wooden fort to explore. Only guide dogs are allowed in the bar. Opening hours are Monday to Saturday 9.30 am to 10 pm, and Sunday 12 noon to 10.30 pm. Telephone: 01892 864209.

How to get there: The pub lies north of the village beside the A26, about 2 miles south of Tunbridge Wells.

Parking: The pub has two large car parks, front and rear.

Length of the walk: 3 miles. Map: OS Landranger 188 Tunbridge Wells (inn GR 357558).

A superlative walk, with fields, woods and views combining to give a memorable experience. It is fun, too, to count the number of homes that bear the Abergavenny emblems.

The Walk
Turn right out of the pub car park and follow the A26 for a short distance until you reach the pretty little church. It was built in 1851 at the cost of the then Earl of Abergavenny and inside the

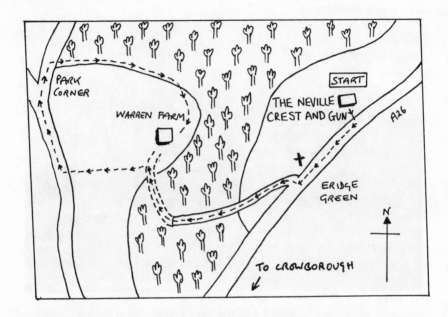

family pews are segregated by a gate across the aisle and have their own entrance at the west end. Turn right into Warren Farm Lane, which winds past a row of modern but tastefully designed cottages. Beyond them stands another cottage that seems to be doing a fair impression of being a castle, battlements and all.

Great rocks rise out from amongst the beech trees to your right as you gently climb the lane to a well marked footpath, the High Weald Walk, on your left. Follow the path and note the tiny bull firmly planted on the roof of Warren Farm. The way lies in a more or less straight line through open countryside for about half a mile, with what seems to be all of Sussex falling away below you. Take a bearing from the white cottage in the distance in front of you. The route enters the line of trees at about eight o'clock and crosses a small stream. Follow the edge of the field and you emerge in a narrow lane via a stile.

Turn right up the lane and try to count the number of rose-decorated tiles that adorn the first house you come to. You pass the round tower of a converted oast house and a proud coat-of-arms on 'Goldsmith' before you reach a road junction and a red telephone box. Turn right here and just beyond Rose Cottage

A rock outcrop near Eridge.

bear right into the trees. It takes you along the fringe of a wood and comes out half a mile further on, on the edge of an open field. Keep going until you reach a track through a scattering of farm buildings, one of which is decorated with a startled-looking gargoyle, and you are back in Warren Farm Lane. If you missed them on the outward journey, look out for the plentiful supply of sweet chestnut trees. From Warren Farm Lane it is just a matter of retracing your steps to return to the pub.

Places of interest nearby

Groombridge Place is three miles south-west of Tunbridge Wells on the B2110. It is a 17th century moated mansion and gardens. Open April and May, bank holidays and weekends only; June 1 to September 30 (daily except Thursday and Friday); October – first two weeks. 2 pm to 6 pm, last admission 5.30 pm. Telephone: 01892 863999.

Mayfield
⑧ The Rose and Crown Inn

The Rose and Crown was reputedly one of the haunts of the Mayfield Gang, notorious smugglers and general ne'er-do-wells of the 18th century. It was here they would hatch plans under the leadership of one Gabriel Tomkins, also known as Joseph Rawlins, Kitt Jarvis and Unkle. Gabriel came to a sticky end eventually, though, hanged in 1750 for robbing the Chester Mail.

Mayfield is renowned for its picturesque qualities – the Victorian writer Coventry Patmore described it as 'the sweetest village in Sussex' – and the Rose and Crown certainly fits into the scheme of things. If you like pubs oozing with period charm, this is for you. It dates from the 16th century and was originally a coaching inn. There are a few simple pew-style seats and an inglenook fireplace in the main bar, which is divided by a wooden screen, and a bar at lower level festooned with hops. Candles top the tables in the restaurant and benches are arranged on the sunny front terrace.

There are three regular ales: Harveys Best, Greene King Abbot and Adnams Bitter, plus a guest ale which changes regularly. The fare ranges from the simple to the sophisticated, and the pub has found its way into several good food guides. Main courses include beef Wellington, Indonesian chicken with fruit and nuts and ratatouille pasta bake for vegetarians. There are daily specials from the chef and you may be lucky enough to encounter a Corsican speciality in chicken breast wrapped in smoked bacon and served with a sauce of garlic, shallots, olives and sun-dried tomatoes. Families are welcome in the dining areas and dogs on a lead in the bar only. The Rose and Crown is open Monday to Friday 11 am to 3 pm, and 5.30 pm to 11 pm; Sunday 12 noon to 3 pm, and 7 pm to 10.30 pm. It is open all day on Saturday.

Telephone: 01435 872200.

How to get there: Mayfield is on the A267 between Heathfield and Tunbridge Wells. The pub is at the eastern end of the High Street, in Fletching Street.

Parking: There is ample parking both at the side and the front of the pub and in the lane.

Length of the walk: 3 miles. Map: OS Landranger 188 Tunbridge Wells (inn GR 270588).

Mayfield perches on a hill, so be prepared for some ups and downs; the scenery all around will more than compensate. There is a crossing of a tributary of the Rother, so tough, waterproof footwear is recommended in winter.

The Walk
Turn right as you leave the pub and then immediately left into East Street. Walk down the hill and then turn left into Southmead Close, staying on the right until you reach a track on the left between two houses leading to a farm gate. Just before the gate turn right on to the footpath which runs behind the houses, pass through the gate into the field and across to the stile opposite and then through the trees. Keep straight ahead beside the hedge down to the bottom of the field where the

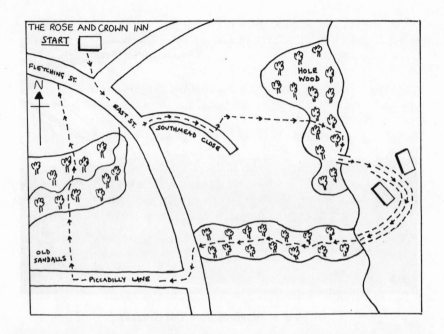

pathway enters Hole Wood. Go downhill through the trees and then along a broad expanse of clear ground to the stream edge. Turn right and you will come to a bridge after about 100 yards.

Cross the stream and then begin to climb the hill on the far bank towards Sharnden Old Manor Farm. Bear right where the path meets the farm track and follow the curve round past the assortment of outhouses. The track does a sort of U-turn and then leads you off to the right for about a quarter of a mile with trees lining the way. It plunges down to the stream, which you cross via stepping stones, and the path rises on the far side and goes past Merrieweathers.

The bridleway becomes a solid track, emerging in the lane near Luckhurst Crouch Farm. Turn left here and then right into Piccadilly Lane. After about 500 yards you reach the turning off to Old Sandalls on the right and the footpath leading down from it, through a copse towards Mayfield, towering above you.

The path crosses a stream and then climbs the hill towards the village, joining it at a convenient point just below Fletching Street. Turn right and continue down the hill until you come to the Rose and Crown on your left.

42

A view of Mayfield from Old Sandalls.

Places of interest nearby

Bartley Mill, Bells Yew Green, near Frant (five miles). A 13th century working watermill. The flour can be bought in the farmshop, and there is also a small museum area, trout hatchery and farm trail. Open all year except between Christmas and New Year's Day, seven days a week. Winter 10 am to 5 pm, summer 10 am to 6 pm. Telephone: 01892 890372.

9 Warbleton
The War Bill-In-Tun

Is this extraordinary name for a pub an appalling pun on the name of the village or, as the story goes, was it provided by an historical event? The more romantic option tells us that centuries ago an impatient soldier came this way and in his greed for beer when he arrived at the alehouse chopped open the barrel with his bill or halberd. Get it? He must have had a good map with him because (apart from all those hyphens) the War Bill-In-Tun is famous for being hard to find. It is a delight to discover though, buried away in the countryside between Heathfield and Hailsham. The old Tudor building, the row of cottages beside it and the church beyond are one of the most attractive collections you will find in the county.

The interior of the pub was extensively renovated about 20 years ago, but it has lost none of its character. There is a small circular bar at one end with steps leading down to a cosy dining room dominated by a massive inglenook fireplace. Here visitors can enjoy a good choice of food freshly prepared and cooked on the premises. Dishes range from the simple, like plough-man's lunch or toasted sandwiches, to the more advanced, like guinea fowl and steak and kidney pie steeped in Guinness. There is always a roast on Sunday and you can follow it with your choice of home-made puddings or ice creams. There are two regular real ales at this freehouse, dispensed by hand pump: Harveys Best Bitter and John Smith's Bitter, backed up by a guest brew. If you can get there early enough you might be able to enjoy a drink in the open air where the handful of wooden benches in the tiny front garden are eagerly snapped up on fine days. Families are welcome and there is no objection to well behaved dogs on a lead. The War Bill-In-Tun is open from 11 am to 3 pm and 7 pm to 11 pm Monday to Saturday and from 12 noon to 2.30 pm and 7 pm to 10.30 pm on Sundays. Telephone: 01435 830636.

How to get there: Complicated. Perhaps the best route is to approach from the B2096 at Punnetts Town, east of Heathfield, and follow the signs south through what seems to be a maze of lanes to the village.

Parking: There is plenty of room for cars at the pub and in the lane outside.

Length of the walk: 3 miles. Map: OS Landranger 199 Eastbourne and Hastings (inn GR 182610).

A delightful walk across undulating, peaceful countryside with wide views, two stream crossings – and an optical illusion at the end of it.

The Walk
Go up the lane towards the church and just beyond the church-yard wall take the path to the left which gives you a good view of the tower. It is a sobering thought that this was a brief prison for local ironmaster Richard Woodman, the most famous of the Sussex martyrs. In the middle of the 16th century he publicly accused the curate of being a religious turncoat, changing from Protestant to Catholic to suit the monarch of the day. He paid dearly for his outspoken views, burnt on a gridiron at Lewes in 1557.

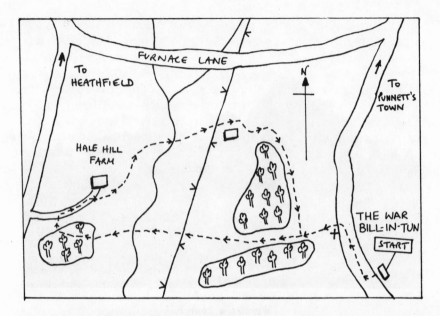

With the church fading in the distance behind you, and Old Heathfield's spire a distant blur to the north, follow the path across a valley with a copse on your left. There are a couple of stiles to negotiate and your way lies clearly across a field, under the power lines striding like giants across the land and down to a stream which eventually feeds the Cuckmere. Pause on the wooden bridge and note how rusty the iron-rich Sussex earth makes the water appear.

It is an easy climb up the other side, with grand views southwards, and you pass through a small copse before gazing down on the track that leads to Hale Hill Farm. Join the track and where it kinks to approach the farm buildings bear off to the right across a field with a barn to your left. Go through the gate at the end and stick by the edge of the field until you reach another stile with an unusually steep green bank on the far side of it. The route lies back across the stream again and on this particular bridge it might be as well to travel one at a time if you are in a party – it is decidedly bouncy in the middle! Exercise a little caution, too, when you reach the end of the field on the far side. The way lies through what appears to be somebody's garden and on our visit was inhabited by a family of goats.

46

Warbleton church.

Over the next stile (it is in the middle of a holly hedge) you turn right and cling to the edge of the field as it swings round beside a wood. Over on your left is the optical illusion. Only the top of Warbleton church tower is visible above the rounded hill in front of it, looking like some mastless galleon floating in the sky. At the top of the slope you rejoin the path that runs from the church and retrace your steps to the pub.

Places of interest nearby
St George's Vineyard, Waldron, near Heathfield. A pretty vineyard of 20 acres with an 11th century barn. Visitors can adopt a vine and receive a personalised bottle of wine. Open March to December. Telephone: 014353 2156.

10 Chiddingly
The Gun

This old inn is an echo from the days when Sussex was the
nation's workshop. It takes its name from one of the products
of an era when armaments, and just about everything else,
were churned out by the county's iron industry. It is hard to
believe that for centuries the county must have looked like
some vision of hell, with fires blazing everywhere and a
constant din, especially in a place now as tranquil as Gun Hill.
It is one of the spots that puts the village of Chiddingly on a par
with mighty Rome – both stand on seven hills; the other half-
dozen are Stone Hill, Thunders Hill, Burgh Hill, Holmes Hill,
Scrapers Hill and Pick Hill.

The Gun dates back to the 15th century and was originally a
farmhouse which brewed and sold its own beer. It retains the
status of a true inn, with a choice of attractive bedrooms
available. The beamed main bar has an old-fashioned Aga in the
corner and a floor of ancient bricks. There are two comfortable
dining areas where fish dishes are one of the specialities of

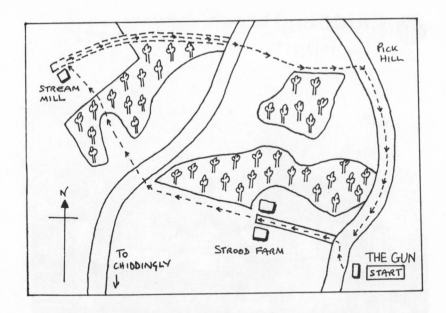

the house – the range is wide and includes Sussex Smokie
(haddock in white wine with wholegrain mustard sauce) and
fresh plaice from Newhaven. There is jumbo steak and kidney
pudding, deep-fried Camembert with gooseberry sauce and a
vegetable delight in Parsnips Molly Parkin – fresh parsnips in
a robust tomato creation covered with cheese and mustard
sauce. There is a more comprehensive selection in the evenings,
including a seafood platter, fillet steak Wellington and vegetable
lasagne. Beer lovers will appreciate the choice offered at this
freehouse: Harveys, Boddingtons, Flowers and Larkins. There is
Heineken and Stella Artois lager, Murphy's and Guinness.

Children are welcome indoors, with their own menu, and are
provided with a safe play area with swings in the pub's spacious
beer garden. They will be fascinated (grown-ups, too) by the
unusual sculpture outside the front door. A man appears to be
floating in a giant barrel, constantly and contentedly spewing
water from his mouth. Weekday opening times are from
11 am to 3 pm, and from 6 pm to 11 pm. The same applies on
Saturday and on Sunday the hours are 12 noon to 3.00 pm and
7.00 pm to 10.30 pm.

Telephone: 01825 872361.

The stone spire of Chiddingly church.

How to get there: The Gun lies to the north-east of Chiddingly. Follow the sign for the village from the A22 at Golden Cross, take the first right and then the second left and you will come to the pub on your right after about a mile.

Parking: There is a large car park at the front and to one side of the pub.

Length of the walk: 3 miles. Map: OS Landranger 199 Eastbourne and Hastings (inn GR 143563).

This is a pleasant stroll combining rolling, open farmland and woods where, in the spring, you will encounter a dense carpet of bluebells.

The Walk

Turn right into the lane outside the pub and then almost immediately go left along the track leading to Strood Farm. There are distant views in front of you of the stone spire of Chiddingly church. There are only three of stone in Sussex and this is the best, 130 feet high. When the vane was regilded in the

1890s an adventurous local without the word 'vertigo' in his vocabulary climbed to the top of the spire and balanced on his head on the apex.

After the farm, go through a gate and you will shortly see the white, timbered rear of Bull River Farm, where the path crosses a lane. The route is clearly signposted across a pair of fields where it plunges into Mill Wood and continues among the trees for about 300 yards. Come out at a stile and look for its twin in front of you on the other side of the field at Stream Mill Farm, which has a reminder of the iron industry in a pond bay and nearby Forge Wood. From here you bear right and follow the tree-lined track as it gently crests the hill and crosses the lane into an apple orchard on the right and strawberry fields on the left.

The way is broad and drops down to a stream with a solid wooden bridge and the most energetic part of the walk beyond it – a steep but brief climb up the edge of a field to a further stile and easy going on the lane at Pick Hill. Turn right and continue along the lane for about a quarter of a mile when you will see the Gun on your left.

11 Milton Street
The Sussex Ox

There are two theories about the identity of the Ox's ghost, a shadowy figure which has been spotted on the landing of this beautiful old building. One, that it is the spirit of a butcher (the pub was a butcher's shop until 80 years ago); the other that it is a phantom smuggler. Because in addition to occupying an idyllic spot at the foot of the downs, the Sussex Ox is convenient for the river Cuckmere, a popular route in times gone by for bringing contraband inland by boat, and close to Alfriston – whose highly organised smuggling activities made it notorious in the 18th century.

Today the pub is a mecca for walkers and lovers of good food, particularly fish. A complete range is available, from pan-fried king prawns to home-made mariner's pot. For land-lubbers, steak, ale and mushroom pie is a popular choice, the Sussex Ox Burger (made to the pub's own recipe) puts fast food in the shade, and vegetarians are well catered for with the likes of broccoli and Stilton quiche. If you choose you can enjoy your meal away from the main bar in the 'Harness Room' restaurant. A stable door leads through to the comfortable 'Sty' family room, while outside there is a large garden with a play area. Harveys Best Bitter, Abbot Ale, Greene King IPA Bitter and Brakspear Bitter are the four regular real ales on offer, with Guinness, lagers and cider also available. The pub is open Monday to Saturday 11 am to 3 pm and 6 pm to 11 pm; and on Sundays from 12 noon to 3 pm, and 7 pm to 10.30 pm.

Telephone: 01323 870840.

How to get there: Milton Street lies south of the A27 between Lewes and Eastbourne. The turning for the hamlet is roughly midway between Wilmington crossroads and the roundabout beside Drusilla's Zoo Park.

Parking: There is a large car park in front of the pub.

Length of the walk: 2 miles. Map: OS Landranger 198 Brighton and the Downs (inn GR 040535).

The South Downs are one of the most spectacular natural features in Britain and this walk also takes in one of the most spectacular made by man, the Long Man of Wilmington. The line of hills stretches from Eastbourne to Winchester, a well-rounded Mother Earth drowsing between the Weald and the sea, and East Sussex can justly boast some of the best 'true' downland – short-cropped turf and an almost treeless skyline.

The Walk

Leave the pub car park and bear right. After about 50 yards, where the lane starts to double back on itself, you will see a pathway off to the right. It climbs gently, flanked by high hedgerows, to the lane above Wilmington village. Bear left as you cross the road and follow the path up on to the downs. Looking back you will see the Sussex Ox far below you and a large chunk of the county spread before you like a feast on a plate. To the west is Firle Beacon – hopefully you will have chosen a fine day when the summit is visible because the old saying 'When Firle Beacon wears a cap, we in the valley gets a drap' is as true a forecaster of imminent rain as any space satellite.

The expanse of water below you in the middle distance is Arlington Reservoir, with the spire of the village church nearby. Depending on the weather, you should be able to spot at least two other spires reaching up from the fields and woods. This is the steepest bit of the climb and it is sure to be punctuated by the song of the skylark; you may see the brilliant colours of goldfinches flitting between the bushes, and perhaps wheatears. They became scarce in centuries past when they were considered a table delicacy.

About 400 yards above the road you come to a gate on your left and the reassuring knowledge that it is downhill all the way from now on. The path takes you round the side of Windover Hill into the awesome presence of the Long Man of Wilmington. This faceless outline of a man carved into the chalk towers above the village which gave him a name. At 227 feet in height with two staves in his hands slightly longer than himself, he is the biggest representation of a human figure in Western Europe but remains a complete mystery. Was he created by the monks at the nearby priory? Is he of Roman origin? Or do his roots lie in the Neolithic period? There are many theories about his identity, from a giant killed on this spot by a hammer tossed by another who lived at Firle, to an ancient god throwing open the gates of dawn. Unlike the Cerne Giant in Dorset he is sexless, gazing sightless and serene across the Weald.

The path leads down from the feet of the Long Man to rejoin the road at Wilmington Priory, picturesque ruins dating partly from the 13th century. It was an 'alien' house, belonging to the Abbey of Grestain in Normandy, and was frequently seized during the wars with the French, and suppressed in 1414 in common with all the other alien houses. It eventually fell into ruin, but what remains is administered by the Sussex Archaeological Trust.

Next to it stands the village church and the route back to the Sussex Ox, but it is well worth making a minor detour down the single street to admire one of the finest small villages in the county. Enter the churchyard through the gate and pass beneath one of the oldest yew trees in Sussex. Its 23 foot girth is now supported by posts and chains, and it is humbling to think that the tree was growing before the arrival of the Conqueror. Inside the church is another curiosity – 'the Wilmington Madonna'.

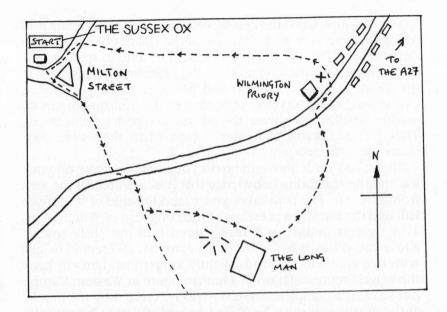

She was removed to the chancel from an exterior wall and her strange, gargoyle-like appearance has led to the suggestion that she could have pre-Christian origins as a pagan fertility symbol.

The path goes diagonally across the churchyard to a gate, beyond which stands a stone seat in memory of the artist Harold Swanick and his wife who lived in the village for many years. Mistletoe grew in the apple trees of their garden at Street Farm. The footpath is clearly defined, leading across fields to the cluster of buildings at Milton Street. When you reach the lane, turn left and then bear right to find yourself back at the Sussex Ox.

Places of interest nearby

Drusillas, on the A27 at Alfriston between Lewes and Eastbourne (one mile). A comprehensive collection of monkeys, penguins, llamas, parrots and other animals and birds. There is also a farmyard, miniature railway and adventure playland. Open all year, daily. Summer months 10 am to 5 pm; winter months 10.30 am to 4 pm. Closed on December 25 and 26. Telephone: 01323 870234. *Michelham Priory*, Upper Dicker (four miles). A large moat and 14th century gatehouse enclose a fine 13th

Looking west towards Firle Beacon.

century priory with Tudor additions. Open from March to October daily, 11 am to 5.30 pm. Telephone: 01323 844224.
Alfriston Clergy House, the Tye, Alfriston. This beautiful 14th century building beside the church and green was the first property acquired by the National Trust in 1896. Open April to October, daily, 10.30 am to 5 pm or sunset if earlier. Telephone: 01323 870001.

12 East Dean
The Birling Gap Hotel

The Victorians loved the seaside. They loved their creature comforts, too, and this place embodies both. It looks like some rambling colonial mansion, verandas and all, that has been scooped up from a tea plantation in India and planted on the very edge of Sussex. All on one level (there are only two steps in the building), it stands yards from the edge of the cliff with breathtaking views out to sea. It was built on the instructions of the Duke of Devonshire and recently celebrated its centenary – but only time will tell if it is still around 100 years from now. Cliff erosion, sometimes at the alarming rate of two feet a year, puts the Birling Gap Hotel in a precarious position so enjoy it while you can. Film star Kevin Costner apparently fell in love with it when he was filming a sequence for *Robin Hood, Prince of Thieves* on the beach, and it was used by the cast of the TV drama *The Life and Loves of a She-Devil* when they were shooting just up the road at the old Belle Tout lighthouse.

Inside, the bar is decorated with old farm implements and

offers an ever-changing range of guest ales to support the regulars John Smith's, Ruddles and Courage. Featured lagers are Holsten, Fosters and Carlsberg. As you might expect, the sea's offerings are prominent on the menu and the Birling Gap Hotel prides itself on seafood specialities which include lobster and crab, plaice and cod, scampi and whitebait. There are also home-made pies and a wide choice in puddings, all to be enjoyed in the large separate dining room. Roast meals are a tradition on Sundays.

Children are welcome and are provided with their own play room complete with a range of games, and dogs are not a problem. You can stay the night, if the fancy takes you, with ten double bedrooms available. Opening hours at the pub are Monday to Saturday 10.30 am to 3 pm and 6 pm to 11 pm; and on Sundays 12 noon to 3 pm and 7 pm to 10.30 pm.

Telephone: 01323 423197.

How to get there: The village of East Dean lies on the sea side of the A259 between Eastbourne and Seaford. Continue through the village along Birling Gap Road and when it takes a 90-degree turn to avoid going over the cliff you will see the Birling Gap Hotel.

Parking: There is a large car park between the hotel and the row of old coastguard cottages which stand opposite it.

Length of the walk: 2 miles. Map: OS Landranger 199 Eastbourne and Hastings (inn GR 962552).

The Seven Sisters are a line of undulating chalk cliffs running west from Birling Gap. The Sisters all have names: Haven Brow, Short Brow, Rough Brow, Brass Point, Flagstaff Point, Bailey's Brow and Went Hill Brow, and this walk will put you on familiar terms with three of them. This beautiful stretch of coastline is owned by the National Trust, some 700 acres in all, and so will remain one of the few undeveloped areas of Sussex by the Sea. It is worth mentioning that these cliffs are high and there is no protective fence between the walker and a drop to certain doom. So keep children and dogs firmly under control and if heights make you giddy, walk well on the land side of the well-worn cliff path.

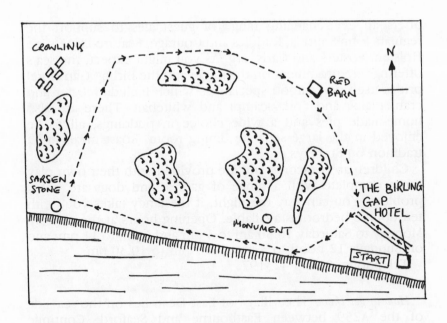

The Walk

From the car park, take the track that leads west with the Birling Gap on your left. At the first opportunity take the clearly marked footpath to your left which takes you on to the springy downland turf and leads to the cliff edge where the path stretches clearly before you. Shortly you will see a monument on your right in the Michel Dean valley, which stares out at the English Channel and bears testament to a brother's sorrow and pride. The inscription reads: 'Michel Dean was bequeathed to the National Trust by W.A. Robertson in memory of his brothers Norman Cairns Robertson, Capt 2nd Batt Hampshire Regt, who died June 20, 1917, at Hanover, Germany, and of Laurance Grant Robertson, 2nd Lieut, 2nd Batt King's Own Scottish Borderers, who was killed in action in France during the Battle of the Somme in or near Delville Wood, 30th July, 1916.'

The undulations of this stretch of the Seven Sisters are like a rollercoaster only, happily, you can pick your own speed and enjoy the sensation of countryside on one side of you and breathtaking space where the sea meets the sky on the other. Turn your eyes earthwards and you may find viper's bugloss, an

59

The Seven Sisters from the Birling Gap.

exotic little plant that flourishes in these parts. Something much larger is the sarsen stone at Flagstaff Point, a massive boulder presented by Viscount Gage of Firle. It was erected on this windy clifftop by the Society of Sussex Downsmen to mark the generosity of William Charles Campbell, whose donation to the Seven Sisters Preservation Fund largely helped purchase the Crowlink Valley in the 1920s 'for the use and enjoyment of the nation'.

The cellars of Crowlink House were reputedly the store for 'Genuine Crowlink' – a smuggled gin which fetched a high price. At Flagstaff Point the last serious skirmish between the smugglers and the authorities took place in 1782 when two 'gentlemen' and one exciseman were killed.

At the sarsen stone turn your back to the sea and head inland for about 500 yards before following a path off to your right and running parallel with the shoreline below you. Keep the Red Barn (no prizes for guessing how it got its name) to your left and continue eastwards for about a quarter of a mile. The path then gently drops down towards the flinty track you first set out on, with the Birling Gap Hotel on your right.

Places of interest nearby

Seven Sisters Sheep Centre, Birling Manor Farm, East Dean (one mile). Visitors can see the various aspects of working with sheep at different times of the year – lambing, shearing and sheep milking. It is open March to September, 2 pm to 5 pm. Telephone: 01323 423302. *The Living World*, Seven Sisters Country Park at Exceat (three miles). This is a natural history exhibition with living displays of native and exotic insects in natural settings, housed in two restored barns. Exhibits include tropical butterflies and moths, mantids and stick insects, and marine and freshwater aquaria. Open all year. Telephone: 01323 870100.

13 Wartling
The Lamb Inn

The village perches compact and pretty above the billiard table green of Pevensey Levels and the Lamb is at the hub of it, serving folk in these parts for some 200 years. The white-painted pub with its ten front windows stands high up from the lane and the entrances are reached by a short flight of steps – a reminder that the wet country and flooding are not far away.

Log fires blaze in the two beamed bars in the winter and there is a games room at the back of the building. An outhouse has been converted into a separate carvery/à la carte restaurant. Bar snacks range from ingenious home-made soups to steak and kidney pie, or you might want to choose from the specials board which changes daily: roast rack of lamb with redcurrant sauce perhaps (a speciality in this sheep country which gave the pub its name) or veal in an almond and spinach sauce. It is a disaster for those with a waistline to guard because there are no fewer than ten puddings to tempt you. A three-course carvery meal is served at lunchtime on Sunday, but note that there is no

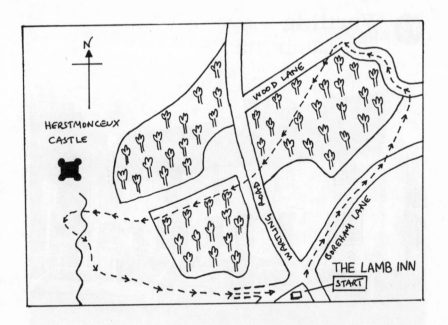

food available on Sunday evenings or at lunchtime on Mondays. Fullers London Pride, Charrington IPA and Draught Bass are the real ales available at this freehouse, supported by Guinness, lagers and cider. Outside there are benches on the terrace, and children and pets are welcome. The Lamb Inn is open Tuesday to Saturday 11 am to 2 pm (3 pm in summer) and 6.30 pm to 11 pm. Sunday 12 noon to 2 pm (3 pm in summer) and 7 pm to 10.30 pm. Closed Monday lunchtime but open 7 pm to 11 pm.
    Telephone: 01323 832116.

How to get there: Wartling is signposted south from the A271 at Boreham Street and north from the roundabout at the junction of the A27 and the A259.

Parking: The pub has its own car park and any overspill can be absorbed in the lanes which run at the front and to the side.

Length of the walk: 3½ miles. Map: OS Landranger 199 Eastbourne and Hastings (inn GR 098652).

Herstmonceux Castle.

The walk provides an opportunity to see Herstmonceux Castle at close quarters, built in 1441 by Sir Roger Fiennes and one of the earliest important brick buildings in the country. Along the way there are peaceful country lanes and woodland carpeted with bluebells in the spring.

The Walk

From the front of the pub walk down the lane and turn right into Boreham Lane. After about three-quarters of a mile you will see a stile on your left. Cross the field, sticking close to the left-hand boundary and exit into the lane on the far side. Turn left and climb to the top of the hill. Just after the road junction turn left on to the signed footpath into the woods, keeping a straight course.

You cut through Wartling Wood for about a quarter of a mile before reaching Wartling Road which you cross to join the signed bridleway on the right-hand side of a car park. Cross the drive that leads to the observatory and maintain a straight line, with the rosy-red grandeur of the castle to your right, to reach a farm gate. Cross the field as far as the finger-post then veer left down to the stile. Continue to the boundary hedge, following it round to a stile, climb over into the field and bear left by the large oak up the incline to a stile.

Head for the stile in the right-hand boundary of the field and then head for the footpath to the right of the wall. Follow it round the field to a stile and along the grassy path beside the garden. One last stile to climb on to a track and then turn left up the drive to the lane and left again back to the Lamb Inn.

Places of interest nearby

Pevensey Castle at Pevensey is just three miles away between Eastbourne and Hastings. These are the impressive remains of fortifications built by Romans, Saxons and Normans to guard the shoreline which has long retreated away from the village. Open all year. Telephone: 01323 762604.

Bodle Street Green
The White Horse Inn

There have been some formidable landlords here in the past. Edward Pankhurst was in charge in the 1880s and brewed his own beer and cider, but despite the thirsty farmworkers it was not enough to make a living. So Mr Pankhurst opened a wheelwright's shop as well. The combined operation still fell short of his expectations with the unhappy result that he went bankrupt. But when the bailiffs called the landlord was a match for them, offering so much hospitality that they fell into a drunken stupor and he was able to move all the tools of his trade to a place of safety before they woke up. The large white horse painted on the tiled roof of the pub originally depicted a racehorse owned by a director of the Star Brewery, then the owners. It had to be removed during the Second World War in case it was used as a guide for German bombers. When the horse was put back in peacetime it was painted facing the opposite way.

The present White Horse Inn dates from 1850, replacing an earlier building which stood 50 yards away which, with the

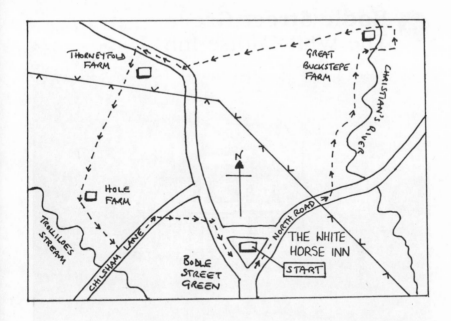

exception of the cellars, was demolished in 1886. One half of the bar is devoted to traditional pub games and the other to dining, with an open fire to keep customers warm in winter. Home-cooked food is served all week except on Mondays when the pub is closed all day. There is a wide-ranging menu which includes a steak and kidney pie reputed to contain a pint of cider and a pint of Guinness. Cottage pie, lasagne and macaroni cheese are among the other dishes on offer. There is a separate menu for children. The well-stocked bar includes two real ales in Harveys Sussex Bitter and Worthington Bitter. In fine weather you can sit out at the picnic tables on the flower-covered terrace. This is very much a family pub and pets can come too. The Lamb Inn is open Tuesday to Saturday 12 noon to 3 pm and 7 pm to 11 pm; and Sunday 12 noon to 3 pm and 7 pm to 10.30 pm.

Telephone: 01323 833243.

How to get there: The village lies north of the A271 and is well signposted from Windmill Hill.

Pathway leading down to Hole Farm.

Parking: You can park behind the bar, in the village hall car park opposite or in the lane.

Length of the walk: 3 miles. Map: OS Landranger 199 Eastbourne and Hastings (inn GR 141655).

Christian's river got its name in the 17th century when it was used for full immersion baptisms. The early part of the walk runs alongside this peaceful stream, while the Nunningham stream is the feature on the return leg.

The Walk

Leave the pub by turning left into North Road. Just beyond the point where the pylon cables pass overhead enter the field through the farm gate on the left and cross to the gate opposite. Keep straight on, making for the house in the distance and then bear left up to a gate and turn right on to the drive passing between the barn and the house. Just before reaching a bridge cross the grass on the left and enter the meadow with Christian's river on your right.

On reaching the boundary to Great Buckstepe Farm bear right, go over the stream and join the bridleway north around the farm, following the driveway up to meet the lane. Keep climbing until you reach a gate on the left marked Thorneyfold Farm. Walk down the drive to the gate in the wall, cross the garden and go into the field at the back. Bear left over the stile to the corner.

Carry straight on close to the field boundary, over a pair of stiles and then bear slightly left across the field making for the stile in the bottom hedge. Continue to the gap in the hedge opposite and then across to the gates, out to the track at Hole Farm, turning left. Walk past the converted mill, turning left on to the tarred drive and then left again when you reach the lane with the Nunningham stream gurgling away to the right of you.

Stick to the lane for about quarter of a mile when you will reach a stile on the right. Climb the bank and bear left across the field, through the open gateway and make for the right of the barn, leaving by the stile into the lane and turn right to return to the White Horse Inn.

Places of interest nearby
The Thomas Smith Trug Shop can be found three miles away at Herstmonceux. Watch the craftsmen at work, creating the famous baskets from strips of wood. Open all year. Telephone: 01323 832137.

15 Witherenden Hill
The Kicking Donkey

There are still a few old timers at Witherenden Hill who can remember the days when you could buy both beer and beef at the Kicking Donkey. This old pub, dating back to the days when Queen Victoria was just a slip of a girl, used to double-up as a butcher's shop. The meaty side of the business did not disappear until 1925, when it became exclusively a pub. And a country pub it very much remains, with no airs and graces. If you are looking for a no-nonsense hostelry, just as grandad might have been accustomed to, then look no further.

Set high up in the Weald, it is about as far away from towns of any kind as you can get in East Sussex. The surroundings are rural and the pub is totally authentic, with a spartan but comfortable main bar, benches that spill across the lane outside to a lawn beside the hopfield and even a veranda where you can sup a pint and enjoy the spectacular views. But the Kicking Donkey is far from behind the times. Where else in England do they boast links with a Dutch cricket team? Every year they come to play the local teams on the pub's own pitch in Pear Tree Lane. The Kicking Donkey has its own cricket team too, of course.

The food is simple and wholesome: home-made soups, assorted sandwiches, snacks and ploughman's lunches. As a freehouse, the pub stocks a wide range of real ales, and it was one of the first in the county to sell Level Best Bitter, brewed at Northiam with Northiam hops. Other beers include Harveys, Boddingtons, Directors and Morland Old Speckled Hen, while there is Heineken and Stella Artois for those who like something lighter in colour, Murphy's and Guinness for those who do not. Children are made welcome in the side bar area and there is great fun to be had on the simple range of play equipment facing the pub. Well behaved dogs can roam wherever they want. The pub is open all day from Monday to Saturday, 11 am to 11 pm, and on Sunday from 12 noon to 2.30 pm and 7 pm to 10.30 pm.

Telephone: 01435 883379.

How to get there: Witherenden Hill is technically at Burwash Common between the A265 Heathfield to Burwash road and the little village of Stonegate to the north. Turn off the main road at Burwash Common, following the sign for Stonegate station, and the Kicking Donkey is about a mile down the lane, on your left.

Parking: There is plenty of room for cars in front and to the side of the pub.

Length of the walk: 2 miles. Map: OS Landranger 188 Tunbridge Wells (inn GR 266641).

Things seem to move at a slightly gentler pace in this part of the world so this walk is for those who do not want to stray more than half a mile from the pub and yet have the benefit of distant vistas all around them.

The Walk

Cross the road from the pub and slightly to the left is a track leading down to Woodknowle Farm. It is easy, level going on a solid surface with Long Wood and Wet Wood below you on the right and the ridge of Coppers Hill, leading to Burwash,

71

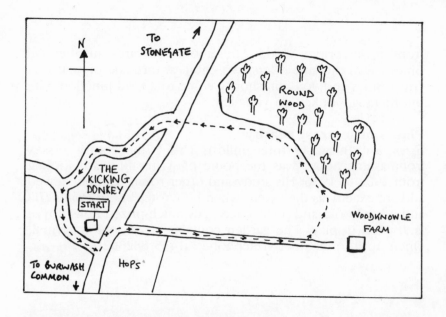

beyond them in the distance. After about a quarter of a mile, just before you reach the range of farm buildings, there is a turning to the left (unmarked, but the first available gap you come to) which you follow, skirting the edge of the field and running alongside Round Wood. The path suddenly veers away from the wood and crosses the field in a straight line to a stile. Clamber over and you emerge on the lane that leads down to Stonegate.

There is a house in the village which was the subject of eerie goings-on at the turn of the century. New owners found there was a particular room with an icy chill on even the hottest of days, and the strange sensation of being watched from behind by some invisible presence – whichever way they were facing. They thought a complete redecoration would improve the atmosphere and this included calling in the chimney sweep. He made an odd discovery. Stuffed high up inside the chimney were a pair of bloodstained sheets. They were burned and the room's chill – and the invisible watcher – vanished from that day onwards.

Take the lane directly opposite and look down in the valley to your right, where the embryonic river Rother meanders in front of Newbridge Wood. After about 300 yards, just beyond Bines Farm, the lane offers two choices: turn sharply left past Great Bines and you will shortly come to a road junction with the Kicking Donkey on your left.

Places of interest nearby
Bateman's, Burwash (three miles). This 17th century Sussex ironmaster's house was the home of writer Rudyard Kipling from 1902 to 1936. His study and other rooms can be viewed and are exactly as they were when he wrote *Puck of Pook's Hill* and other books and poems here. His much-prized Rolls Royce is also on display. The garden contains a restored watermill. Open April to October. Telephone: 01435 882302.

⑯ Three Leg Cross, Ticehurst
The Bull

The Bull has been a pub for about 100 years, but this delightful building has been around a lot longer than that. It was constructed between 1385 and 1425 and was originally a Wealden hall house – making it one of the oldest dwelling places, bar castles, in the county. What the Victorians decided to cover up has been revealed in its full glory in recent years, the plaster stripped away to show the original wattle and daub walls. Everything revolves around the giant chimney in the centre of the pub, its back-to-back fireplaces providing the warmth in both bars. The furniture fits the atmosphere of the place with an assortment of long wooden tables, old kitchen chairs and pew bench seats, and the beamed ceilings are festooned with garlands of hops.

Cider lovers will be interested to know this freehouse stocks a local brew, Long Man Cider, and for the real-ale devotees there is Harveys Best, Fullers London Pride, Morland Old Speckled Hen, Level Best and Bull Bitter specially brewed by

Bass. The food here is highly imaginative. Bar meals are chalked on blackboards and rubbing shoulders with the ploughman's and the home-made soup you might find goat's cheese in filo pastry or spring rolls filled with sardines. There's a separate dining room where you can sample dishes from a more comprehensive menu, featuring such delights as Caribbean chicken (chicken breast pan-fried with coconut milk, mangoes, lime and fresh ginger) or salmon strudel (wrapped in filo pastry with a hint of Pernod and baked in a watercress sauce). Outside there is a large beer garden stocked with wooden benches, and children will love the ornamental fishpond. You can go Gallic and try your hand on one of the pub's two petanque pitches. Opening hours are Monday to Saturday 11 am to 3 pm and 6 pm to 11 pm, and Sunday 12 noon to 3 pm, and 7 pm to 10.30 pm.

Telephone: 01580 201289.

How to get there: Ticehurst straddles the B2087 road between Wadhurst and Hawkhurst. Three Leg Cross lies about half a mile to the north and the lane leading to it is at the western end of Ticehurst High Street.

Parking: There is ample room for vehicles in the pub's own car park, and the adjacent lanes can accommodate any overspill.

Length of the walk: 3 miles. Map: OS Landranger 188 Tunbridge Wells (inn GR 686312).

This walk takes you to admire Bewl Water, the largest area of inland water in the south-east and alive with wildfowl. Along the way tantalising vistas open up in this unspoilt corner of the county.

The Walk
Leave from the front of the pub and take the lane to your left. Ignore the turning to Tinkers Lane and continue for about 50 yards until you see a turning on your left marked Hazelhurst Farm. Follow this solid track and you can't really go wrong because East Sussex County Council has expertly signposted and maintained the route around the water. When you come to a junction, just as the placid expanse of Bewl comes into view,

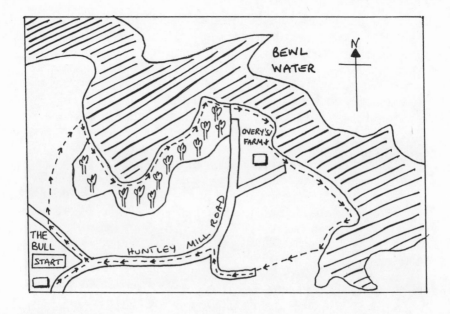

take the right-hand path marked 'Bridleway and Water Walk' and simply follow it through the trees and open spaces hugging this jagged inlet.

When you emerge from the copse just before Overy's Farm it is worth reflecting that the far shore in front of you is Kent and that somewhere in the stretch of water between lies the county boundary. The geese and ducks are totally cosmopolitan in their lifestyle, holding no allegiance to either county. Particularly attractive are the Canada geese, waddling in great clucking herds and not the least perturbed by the presence of humans.

If you have had enough when you come to the lane beside Overy's Farm, simply continue in a straight line back along Huntley Mill Road, with its distinctive line of poplar trees, and ignore the next paragraph.

Stouter spirits should continue to follow the water path as it twists in a gradual arc to the right, with a distant view of Rosemary Lane where it forms a causeway across Bewl. It runs beside another inlet and at the point where the water has to give way to dry land there is a bridlepath marked for Three Leg Cross on your right. Follow this wooded way for about a quarter of

Bewl Water.

a mile and twist right when offered an option into Huntley Mill Road. Turn left and enjoy the distant views of Ticehurst and its church on your left for a quarter of a mile until you return to the hamlet and the Bull.

Places of interest nearby
Pashley Manor Gardens, Pashley Manor, Ticehurst (one mile). Gardens created in the true English romantic style in the 18th century surround a Grade I ironmaster's house 300 years older. The gardens extend over eight acres with many ancient trees and shrubs, a waterfall and a moat. Open April to October Tuesday to Thursday, Saturday and bank holidays 11 am to 5 pm. Telephone: 01580 200692. *Merriments Gardens*, Hawhurst Road, Hurst Green (four miles). A four-acre garden featuring herbaceous borders, unusual plants, water gardens, orchard and woodland. Open April to September daily, 10 am to 5 pm. Telephone: 01580 860666.

⑰ Salehurst
The Salehurst Halt

The Eight Bells is not the commonest of pub names, but this parish had two within a mile of each other. Prefixing the name with 'old' and 'new' did not really solve the problem of people getting them muddled up. Something had to give and 17 years ago the original Eight Bells changed its name – and kept alive memories of the area's lost railway, a victim of Dr Beeching's axe, by becoming the Salehurst Halt. The original halt was on the now dismantled line about 40 yards behind the pub, and was a popular embarkation point for farmers and churns of milk. It gets muddy in the Rother valley in winter and today you can still see the stepping stones which were installed for passengers to spare their footwear. The pub dates from 1830 and was built on the site of a thatched building destroyed by a fire. It proudly displays the Les Routiers emblem outside and after sampling the food you will understand why it was selected for the listing. The emphasis is always on freshness. There are two different menus to choose from, lunch and dinner, both wide ranging and reasonably priced. If you like you can dine al fresco on the terrace with views across the river valley to Robertsbridge Abbey.

Harveys is always available at the single, cosy bar of this freehouse, supported by an ever-changing selection of guest ales. Children are welcome inside and will love the large rear garden with a stable wall older than the pub itself. There is no objection to dogs, but you may be asked to put them on a lead if they get too frisky. The Salehurst Halt is closed all day on Tuesdays, but open every other day from 12 noon to 3 pm, and 7 pm to 11 pm.

Telephone: 01580 880620.

How to get there: The pub stands in Church Road about a mile east of Robertsbridge. The tiny settlement of Salehurst is well signposted from the A21(T).

Parking: There is ample space at the pub car park and in the lane outside.

Length of the walk: 3 miles. Map: OS Landranger 199 Eastbourne and Hastings (inn GR 249741).

The Garden of England may be a few miles away over the Kent border, but in this part of East Sussex they do a more than fair impersonation. Wander through hopfields and orchards to savour magnificent views of the rounded, wooded countryside.

The Walk
From the pub, turn right towards the pretty church. It is built of Hastings sandstone and inside boasts a 12th century font with a chain of salamanders (the emblem of the Crusaders) crawling around the base of the shaft. Local legend says it was given to the church by King Richard the Lionheart himself – and he had good reason to show his gratitude. It was the Abbot of Robertsbridge who negotiated a deal for the release of the king when he was imprisoned in Austria.

The path lies through the church gates and along the left-hand side of the building through the churchyard, which has a number of interesting tombstones. Turn left when you emerge

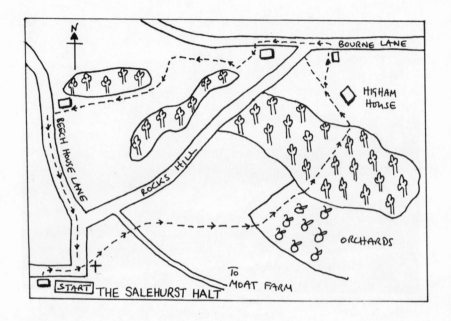

and follow the path round the edge of a pair of hopfields, a forest of poles covered in a lush green canopy in summer, then cross a small lane which leads to Moat Farm. The route is well marked and skirts a broad field before climbing into an orchard. Resist the temptation to sample the produce and stick to the broad path as it rises for about 300 yards and enters a wood on the left. It is a bit like a tunnel, with a fence on either side and great boughs overhead, but it is a tunnel with a light at the end of it and when you emerge in a field turn left and head for the stile in the corner.

This takes you on to the driveway of Higham House, an impressive Victorian mansion. Continue up the driveway for about 100 yards and look back – that statue on the left of the house is uncannily lifelike! Do not be alarmed when the foot-path sign suddenly deviates from the drive and heads into the back of someone's garden, you are on the right track. The owners of Lake Abbot are used to people marching past their duckpond and out of their front gates into a lane. Here you turn left and ignore the road's first turning to the left which comes soon afterwards and leads ultimately back to the pub. It may

Hopfield near Salehurst.

have been quite a climb up from the church, but there is more country to cross and you can content yourself with the knowledge that from now it is downhill all the way.

The footpath lies to the left just beyond Jollie's Farm, and continues downwards through trees and past a small pond for about 500 yards before coming to a stile. Here you branch off sharply right and go downhill across a field and negotiate a bridge over a small stream. Make your own guesses about the origin of the curious lumpy 'causeway' you have to follow – perhaps it was part of some medieval field system. You have to cross another stream before a gentle incline takes you up past woodland to a range of farm buildings and a narrow squeeze between two gardens to Beech House Lane. Turn left and look out for an unusual barn at the side of the road – it stands on stilts. After less than a quarter of a mile the church, and the Salehurst Halt just beyond, will spring suddenly into view.

⑱ Ewhurst Green
The White Dog

This freehouse is a great place for the gourmet and is listed in the Egon Ronay guide. The food in the separate restaurant area is sophisticated but reasonably priced: duck Magret in a mustard and bramble sauce, Din-Din duck in spring onions and ginger, sole fresh daily from Hastings, and wonderful things with skate wings gives you just a flavour of what is on offer. But there is also an appetising bar menu, where the humble ploughman's rubs shoulders with the likes of chicken tikka. There are three real ales available in the winter, Ansells, Harveys and Bass, and in the summer you can add Brakspear to the list. Tennents, Fosters, Carling and Kronenbourg are on offer for lager drinkers, while cider lovers can choose between draught Merrydown and Dry Blackthorn. The White Dog used to be one of the furthest flung outposts in the empire of the now defunct Beard's brewery at Lewes.

The pub dates back 400 years in part, to the brick floor area of the main bar with its giant inglenook fireplace, and used to be called the Castle. This led to confusion with the pub of the same name just across the valley at Bodiam so previous licensees changed the name – they were the proud owners of two Pyrennean mountain dogs. If you are sitting by the fireplace, incidentally, listen out for the pub's mysterious footsteps, a methodical tread coming out from an upstairs room. Bed and breakfast can also be found here, with four en-suite bathrooms and use of the swimming pool in the large rear gardens with magnificent views to Bodiam, the best preserved medieval fortress in the land, and beyond. Children are given a warm welcome and dogs, too. It is worth noting that the restaurant is closed on Sundays and Mondays. The pub is open Monday to Saturday 12 noon to 3.30 pm and 6.30 pm to 11 pm, and Sunday 12 noon to 3 pm and 7 pm to 10.30 pm.

Telephone: 01580 830264.

How to get there: Ewhurst Green is one of the county's more remote villages. It lies roughly halfway between Robertsbridge and Northiam. From the A28 at Horns Cross, south of Northiam, take the Staplecross turning and then follow the signs for Ewhurst Green along Lordine Lane. The pub is in the shadow of the village church.

Parking: There is a big car park to one side of the White Dog.

Length of the walk: 2 miles. Map: OS Landranger 199 Eastbourne and Hastings (inn GR 245795).

This is a village of tremendous charm and in many ways still 'undiscovered'. It occupies an idyllic setting in the county's hilly uplands and the relaxing walk gives a taste of that tranquillity.

The Walk

Turn left outside the pub as though you were walking away from the village and look for the footpath on your right. Go over the stile and make sure you do not miss the bridge and stile on your left after about 200 yards. Follow the path beside the hedge and enter Sempstead Wood via another wooden bridge.

Your way lies through a dense forest of firs and emerges after about 300 yards in a broad woodland ride. Turn right. Continue

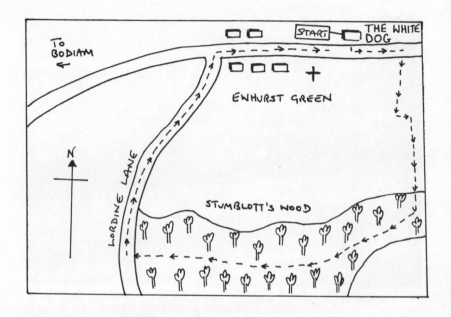

along the path and, without you knowing it, Sempstead Wood somewhere becomes Stumblott's Wood. Enjoy being among the trees for about a quarter of a mile and then you reach a gate and Lordine Lane. Turn right and go over the stream bridge at Stumblott's Farm and up the other side, climbing gently on a quiet road past Watermans Farm and the road to Sogg's House.

It takes you up into the village where you turn right and pass the mixture of old and new houses on either side of the road. Particularly impressive is the imaginative way new cottages have been introduced around the village green.

Next door is the church of St James the Great, with its unusual conical spire and its story of an Edwardian tragedy in the form of a 'corona', or chandelier, and a window within. Five year old William Jacobson drowned in a pond in his father's garden at Lordine Farm in March 1905. In the window he is pictured sitting on Christ's knee with texts that show the grief-stricken parents' efforts to understand their loss. They emptied their dead son's money box and put the contents towards buying the corona for the oil lamps which then lit the church. It hangs in the nave and is now electrified.

The lane below the church at Ewhurst Green.

Just beyond the church, last in the line of this pretty row, is the White Dog.

Places of interest nearby

Great Dixter House and Gardens, Northiam (three miles). A beautiful timber-framed manor house dating from the 15th century. The great hall was restored by Sir Edwin Lutyens, who also designed the gardens which feature topiary and meadow gardens. Open April to October. Telephone: 01797 253160.
Bodiam Castle, Bodiam (one mile). Built in 1385 to withstand a French invasion that never came, Bodiam Castle was 'slighted' in the 17th century and has remained uninhabited ever since. Its walls and towers, reflected in the wide moat, are remarkably well-preserved. The National Trust has established an audio-visual presentation inside on 'Life in a Medieval Castle'. Open all year except from December 25 to 29. Telephone: 01580 830436.

19 Sedlescombe
The Queen's Head

The Queen's Head stands beside the green in the pretty village of Sedlescombe (the Victorian writer Coventry Patmore said it surpassed all others in Sussex, bar Mayfield) and was originally the property of the Abbot of Battle. It was first registered as a trading house in 1523 and in its coaching days was the turning point for the Eastbourne run. The stables still stand at the back of the building, but the old stone horse trough produced by the 'Metropolitan Drinking Fountain and Cattle Trough Association' is a bit of an imposter. It was bought by the landlord in recent years to prevent it being broken up and used as road foundation. Mugs and garlands of hops hang from the ceiling in the comfortable bar, and an array of tables and benches stand on the lawn of the beer garden. At the side of the building is a well stocked aviary which is an instant hit with children.

Strange things happen in the giant fireplace that dominates the beamed interior of this old coaching inn. When landlord John Cook closes for the night he always makes sure that all is well with the fire. The next morning, as often as not, he will come downstairs to the bar and find that items in the fireplace have moved about – the logs are not where he left them or the rich variety of ornaments that adorn the inglenook have mysteriously swapped places.

The inn is a Whitbread pub and you can take your pick from at least four real ales like Flowers Original, Fremlins Bitter, Strong Country Bitter and a guest beer – it's a different one each week from a range of 50. The food is simple but wholesome: hot soup in the winter months, ploughman's lunches, pies and sandwiches. Well behaved children and dogs are welcome here.

The pub is open Monday to Saturday 10 am to 2.30 pm, and 6.30 pm to 11 pm; and Sunday 12 noon to 2.30 pm and 7 pm to 10.30 pm.

Telephone: 01424 870228.

How to get there: Sedlescombe lies off the A21(T) about 6 miles north of Hastings. The A229 road to Staplecross forms the main street of the village.

Parking: There is a large car park to the side of the pub.

Length of the walk: 4½ miles. Map: OS Landranger 199 Eastbourne and Hastings (inn GR 172788).

A longish walk but a rewarding one. It takes in Powdermill Reservoir which keeps alive the memory of a hazardous village industry – making gunpowder. Four men died when the sifting house at the gunpowder mills blew up with a ton of gunpowder inside one morning in December 1764, including James and Thomas Gilmore, the two sons of the proprietor. The reservoir is surrounded by dense old woodland so a stick might be handy to keep the brambles at bay.

The Walk

Turn right as you leave the pub and right again into Brede Lane. Keep going for about a mile, past new houses and into open countryside, until you reach a sharp bend in the road and a stile leading off to the left. Cross the field to the stile in the far corner where you enter Powdermill Lane by the entrance to Jacob's

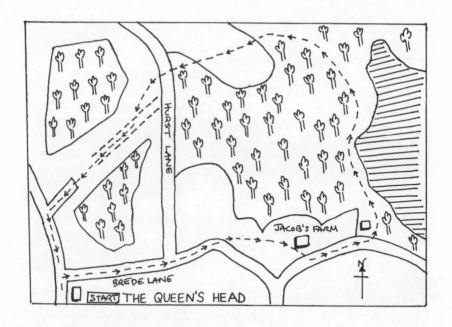

Farm. Turn left and continue down the lane and after passing a house look for a stile on your left.

The path meanders through mature trees to a new plantation and stile to an open area of scrub. There are lovely views of the reservoir twinkling below you to the right. The way leads down over the bridge of a stream feeding Powdermill and then up some steps into the wood. There is a ditch to cross and then the path rises to a stile in the fence. Bear right across the open ground to the stile opposite and re-enter the woods.

There is a path off to the left, indicated by a low marker, which you will come to after a short distance. Wind your way among the trees until you come to a grassy path where you bear left and then left again on to a wide forest track. You reach a farm gate and cross the field beyond in a straight line. Enter the next field on the left and hug the line of the hedge until you reach a stile. Go over and continue along the path to a narrow lane.

Walk straight across and join the signed path opposite. Shortly you reach a gravel road where you turn right and pass a scattering of houses on to a grassy track which narrows and

Powdermill Reservoir.

enters a field. Exit at the stile on to a concrete road, turning left on to a gravel lane, down to the main road and left again back to the Queen's Head.

Places of interest nearby

Battle Abbey, High Street, Battle (four miles). The grounds and ruins of this great Benedictine Abbey, founded by William the Conqueror to commemorate the Battle of Hastings fought on this site in 1066, are open to visitors. The church's high altar supposedly marks the spot where King Harold was killed and there is a well-preserved monks' dormitory and excavated foundations to be seen. Open all year, except December 25 and 26, and January 1. Telephone: 01424 773792. *Battle Town Model Show* and *Almonry Gardens*, The Almonry, High Street, Battle. A scale model of the town accompanied by narration, sound effects and synchronised lighting provide an insight into Battle's history and appeal. Open all year, Monday to Saturday 10 am to 5 pm. Closed January 1, December 25, 26 and bank holiday Mondays. Telephone: 01424 772727.

20 Udimore
The King's Head

Skittles is a rarity in Sussex pubs, but the King's Head has had an indoor alley since 1990. It is a popular free attraction with visitors of all ages. Old records show that a pub stood on this spot as long ago as 1535, though the present building is not that old. It may once have been the gate house to old Court Lodge, a timbered building which stood near the village church, dismantled piece by piece in 1920 and put together again at Groombridge on the Sussex/Kent border – the ultimate in jigsaw puzzles. Certainly pieces of medieval wall are incorporated in the present structure of the King's Head.

Here they are proud that it is a pub where you can get food, not a restaurant where you can get a drink. In the long, comfortable bar you can enjoy a variety of salads, local lamb steaks, steak and ale pie, cod and chips and hot sausage and onions, to name but a few, with everything fresh and cooked on the premises. The Sunday lunches are a byword in the district. The beers on offer at this freehouse include Bentley's Yorkshire

Bitter, Harveys, Butcombe Bitter and guest ales; Guinness is there, of course, and lager lovers can choose between Stella Artois and Heineken. There is no objection to children and to keep them amused on fine days (if they are not playing skittles) there is an elaborate wooden climbing frame in the beer garden. The pub is open Monday to Saturday 11 am to 3 pm and 6 pm to 11 pm; Sunday 12 noon to 3 pm and 7 pm to 10.30 pm.

Telephone: 01424 882349.

How to get there: Udimore lies on the B2089 between Broad Oak (north of Brede on the A28) and Rye.

Parking: The car park extends for about 100 yards from the pub, alongside the main road.

Length of the walk: 3 miles. Map: OS Landranger 199 Eastbourne and Hastings (inn GR 198852).

Udimore (locals will tell you the strange name is derived from the French 'eau de mer' from the days when the sea came a lot closer than it does today) stands on a high ridge with river valleys either side, the Tillingham and the Brede. This walk takes you on the latter with an excursion into the flatland that is guaranteed to blow away the cobwebs, and allows magnificent views across the former on the return trip.

The Walk

The footpath is located directly behind the pub car park. Skirt the edge of the apple orchard and head for the squat tower of St Mary's church. By an ancient edict church fonts were not to be made of wood and the churchwardens here in the 18th century were either too poor or too mean to buy a new one. So they carried out an ingenious forgery on Udimore's strange little pudding bowl font, carefully painting the outside of the wooden bowl like weathered stone and the inside like lead.

Follow the footpath signs and you plunge down the hillside on a flinty track with high banks and trees either side. When you reach the bottom, after about a quarter of a mile, bear right, go over the stile and cross the field to the bridge which spans the river Brede. The views are wonderful, the broad expanse of flat river valley giving way on the far side to the hilly ridge at

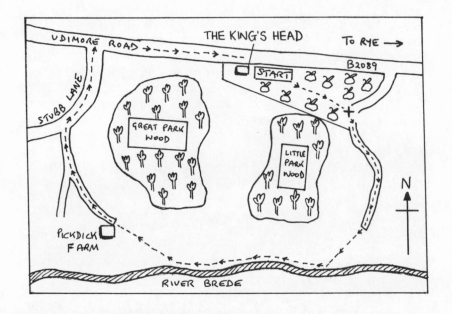

Icklesham. But be warned – the geographical features turn this into a wind tunnel, with a stiff breeze on even the stillest of days. Do not cross the bridge but bear right and follow the edge of the river for about half a mile. You will have the occasional two-carriage train for company on the Rye to Hastings line and hundreds of curious sheep.

Leave the river behind when you see the distinctive twin peaks of a converted oast house halfway up the hillside to your right. Head for the oast and you reach Pickdick Lane, a track running past farm buildings and gently climbing to a junction, where you turn right. Note the house with the American-style mail box. Pickdick Lane joins Stubb Lane after about 300 yards, where you turn right and then right again at the junction of the B2089.

It is exactly a mile to the pub from here, but the road is not particularly busy and the view to the left of the river Tillingham is a delight. As you approach Udimore, note that the village sign is of the old-fashioned variety. Are there any others like it in East Sussex? Shortly afterwards you will reach the King's Head on your right.

The path through the orchard near Udimore.

Places of interest nearby

Lamb House, West Street, Rye (three miles). An early Georgian house which was the home of American writer Henry James from 1898 to 1916 and later of author E.F. Benson of Mapp and Lucia fame. It is owned by the National Trust. Open April to October, Wednesday and Saturday 2 pm to 6 pm. Telephone: 01797 223763.